GROWING

MARIJUANA FOR

BUSINESS

By

DR. JULIE OWENS

Contents

Chapter 1

UNDERSTANDING MARIJUANA CULTIVATION

1. Introduction to marijuana cultivation

Marijuana, also known as cannabis, is a versatile plant with various uses, including medicinal, recreational, and industrial purposes. Cultivating marijuana involves growing the plant either indoors, outdoors, or in a controlled environment. It requires careful attention to environmental factors, nutrient management, and plant health to achieve optimal growth and yield.

Before starting a marijuana cultivation project, it's essential to understand the legal regulations regarding cannabis cultivation in your area. Many regions have specific laws and regulations governing the cultivation, possession, and use of marijuana, so make sure to research and comply with local laws.

The cultivation process typically begins with selecting the right strain of marijuana for your desired outcome. There are numerous strains with different characteristics, such as growth patterns, cannabinoid profiles, and flavors. Consider factors like the plant's height, flowering time, and cannabinoid content when choosing a strain.

Once you've selected a strain, you'll need to prepare your growing space. For indoor cultivation, this might involve setting up a grow room with proper lighting, ventilation, and humidity control. Outdoor cultivation requires selecting a suitable outdoor location with adequate sunlight and soil quality.

Next, you'll need to prepare the soil or growing medium. Cannabis plants thrive in well-draining soil with good aeration. You may also choose to grow in hydroponic systems, which use nutrient-rich water solutions instead of soil.

Nutrient management is crucial for healthy marijuana plants. They require a balanced diet of macronutrients (nitrogen, phosphorus, potassium) and micronutrients (calcium, magnesium, iron) throughout their growth stages. Using organic fertilizers or compost can help provide these nutrients in a natural and sustainable way.

Monitoring and controlling environmental factors like temperature, humidity, and light cycles are critical for successful cultivation. Marijuana plants have specific requirements for each growth stage, so it's essential to adjust these factors accordingly.

Throughout the cultivation process, you'll need to monitor plant health and watch for signs of pests, diseases, or nutrient deficiencies. Early detection and intervention can prevent these issues from affecting your plants' growth and yield.

As your marijuana plants mature, you'll need to consider the timing of harvest. The ideal harvest time varies depending on the strain and desired effects. Harvesting too early or too late can impact the potency and quality of your final product.

After harvest, proper drying and curing are essential steps to preserve the quality and potency of your marijuana buds. This process involves drying the buds slowly in a controlled environment and then curing them in airtight containers to enhance flavor and aroma.

Marijuana cultivation requires knowledge, patience, and attention to detail, but with the right techniques and care, you can cultivate high-quality cannabis at home.

2. History and legal status of marijuana

Marijuana, also known as cannabis, has a long history of use for medicinal, recreational, and industrial purposes. It has been cultivated for thousands of years, with evidence of its use dating back to ancient civilizations in Asia, Africa, and the Middle East. In these early cultures, marijuana was primarily used for its medicinal properties and as a source of fiber for textiles and rope.

In more recent history, marijuana became associated with recreational use, particularly in the 20th century. In the United States, marijuana was initially legal and widely used in the 19th century for medicinal purposes. However, its legal status began to change in the early 20th century with the rise of prohibitionist attitudes and the passage of laws restricting its use.

The Marihuana Tax Act of 1937 effectively made marijuana illegal at the federal level in the United States, leading to its classification as a Schedule I controlled substance under the Controlled Substances Act of 1970. This classification means that marijuana is considered to have a high potential for abuse, no accepted medical use, and a lack of accepted safety for use under medical supervision.

Despite federal prohibition, the legal status of marijuana has evolved in recent years. Many states in the U.S. have legalized marijuana for medical and/or recreational use, either through voter initiatives or legislative action. As of 2022, recreational marijuana is legal in 18 states and the District of Columbia, while medical marijuana is legal in 37 states.

Internationally, the legal status of marijuana varies widely. Some countries, such as Canada, Uruguay, and several European nations, have legalized marijuana for medical and/or recreational use. Others have decriminalized possession of small amounts or have implemented various forms of medical marijuana programs.

The legal status of marijuana varies widely across different countries and jurisdictions. Some countries, such as Canada, Uruguay, and several U.S. states, have legalized marijuana for recreational and medicinal use. In these places, there are regulations governing its production, sale, and consumption.

In other countries, marijuana remains illegal or is only legal for medicinal use under strict regulations. The legal status of marijuana is a complex and evolving issue, with ongoing debates about its potential benefits and risks, as well as the appropriate regulatory frameworks for its use.

3. Types of marijuana plants (sativa, indica, hybrids)

Sativa: Sativa plants are known for their tall, slender stature with long, narrow leaves. They are native to warmer climates and are often grown in equatorial regions. Sativa strains are known for their energizing and uplifting effects, making them popular for daytime use. They are believed to have higher levels of THC (tetrahydrocannabinol), the psychoactive compound in marijuana, compared to CBD (cannabidiol), which contributes to their stimulating effects.

Indica: Indica plants are characterized by their shorter, bushier stature with broader leaves. They are native to cooler climates and are often grown in mountainous regions. Indica strains are known for their relaxing and sedating effects, making them popular for evening or nighttime use. They are believed to have higher levels of CBD compared to THC, which contributes to their calming effects.

Hybrids: Hybrids are created by crossbreeding sativa and indica strains to combine their desirable traits. Hybrid strains can vary widely in their characteristics, depending on the specific genetics of the parent plants. They can exhibit a balance of sativa and indica effects or lean more towards one type depending on the genetic dominance. Hybrids are popular for their ability to offer a wide range of effects and flavors, catering to different preferences and medicinal needs.

4. Basic anatomy of the marijuana plant

Roots: The roots anchor the plant in the soil and absorb water and nutrients from the soil.

Stem: The stem provides support for the plant and transports water, nutrients, and sugars between the roots and the rest of the plant.

Leaves: Marijuana plants have iconic palmate leaves with serrated edges. These leaves are important for photosynthesis, the process by which plants convert light energy into chemical energy.

Nodes: Nodes are the points on the stem where leaves, branches, and buds grow. They are crucial for understanding the plant's growth pattern and for techniques like topping and pruning.

Internodes: Internodes are the spaces between nodes on the stem. The length of internodes can vary depending on the plant's genetics, growing conditions, and stage of growth.

Apical Bud: The apical bud, also known as the terminal bud or apical meristem, is the main growing point at the top of the plant. It produces hormones that regulate the growth of the plant.

Axillary Buds: These are the buds that develop in the leaf axils (the angle between the stem and the leaf). They can grow into branches or flowers (buds) if the plant is allowed to flower.

Flowers (Buds): The flowers, or buds, of the marijuana plant are the reproductive organs where the plant produces cannabinoids and terpenes. These compounds are responsible for the plant's medicinal and psychoactive effects.

Trichomes: Trichomes are tiny, resinous glands that cover the flowers, leaves, and stems of the marijuana plant. They produce cannabinoids and terpenes and play a crucial role in the plant's defense against pests and environmental stressors.

5. Growth stages of marijuana plants (seedling, vegetative, flowering)

Seedling Stage: This is the first stage after germination, lasting for about 1-3 weeks. Seedlings have just emerged from the soil and have their first sets of true leaves. They are delicate and require careful watering and light exposure.

Vegetative Stage: This stage lasts for several weeks to several months, depending on the desired size of the plant. During vegetative growth, the plant focuses on developing a strong root system and lush foliage. It requires ample light, nutrients, and water to support rapid growth.

Flowering Stage: This stage is triggered by changes in the light cycle. When the plant receives 12 hours of darkness and 12 hours of light, it switches from vegetative growth to flowering. Flowering can last 7-14 weeks, depending on the strain. During this stage, the plant produces buds rich in cannabinoids and terpenes.

Chapter 2

SETTING UP YOUR MARIJUANA GROW SPACE

1. Choosing an indoor vs. outdoor grow space

Climate: Outdoor cultivation is influenced by the local climate. If you live in a region with a mild climate and a long growing season, outdoor growing can be a good option. However, if you live in an area with extreme temperatures or frequent inclement weather, indoor cultivation may offer more control over the growing environment.

Control: Indoor cultivation allows for greater control over environmental factors such as temperature, humidity, light, and air circulation. This control can lead to more consistent yields and higher-quality buds. Outdoor cultivation relies more on natural conditions, which can be less predictable.

Space: Indoor cultivation can be done in smaller spaces, such as a closet, tent, or dedicated grow room. This makes it suitable for growers with limited outdoor space or those who want to keep their cultivation discreet. Outdoor cultivation requires a larger open space, such as a backyard or garden plot.

Cost: Setting up an indoor grow space can be more expensive initially, as it requires equipment such as grow lights, ventilation systems, and possibly a grow tent or room. Outdoor cultivation may have lower upfront costs, especially if you have access to a suitable outdoor space with natural sunlight.

Security: Outdoor cultivation may be more vulnerable to theft or detection by authorities, depending on the legality of marijuana cultivation in your area. Indoor cultivation can offer more privacy and security, especially if you take measures to control odors and noise.

Yield: Both indoor and outdoor cultivation can produce high-quality yields, but the potential yield per plant can vary. Indoor plants are generally smaller but can produce dense buds with higher THC levels. Outdoor plants can grow larger but may be more susceptible to pests, diseases, and environmental stressors.

2. Designing an efficient grow room or tent

✓ **Location and Space:**

Choose a location with adequate space for your grow room or tent, considering the number of plants you plan to grow.

Ensure the space is well-ventilated and can accommodate the necessary equipment without overcrowding.

✓ **Lighting:**

Select the appropriate lighting system based on the size of your grow space and the stage of plant growth.

LED grow lights are popular for their energy efficiency, customizable spectrum, and low heat output, but high-pressure sodium (HPS) and metal halide (MH) lights are also used.

✓ Ventilation and Air Circulation:

Install exhaust fans and carbon filters to control temperature, humidity, and odors.

Use oscillating fans to promote air circulation and prevent stagnant air, which can lead to mold and mildew.

✓ Temperature and Humidity Control:

Maintain a consistent temperature range of 70-85°F (21-29°C) during the day and slightly lower at night.

Keep humidity levels between 40-60% during vegetative growth and 40-50% during flowering to prevent mold and bud rot.

✓ Watering and Nutrient Delivery:

Use a reliable watering system, such as drip irrigation or hand-watering with a watering can, to ensure even moisture distribution.

Implement a nutrient delivery system, such as hydroponics or soilless mixes, to provide the necessary nutrients to your plants.

✓ **Growing Medium:**

Choose a growing medium based on your preferred cultivation method (e.g., soil, hydroponics, coco coir).

Ensure the medium is well-draining and provides adequate support for root development.

✓ **CO_2 Enrichment:**

Consider CO_2 enrichment to enhance plant growth and yield, especially in enclosed environments.

Monitor CO_2 levels and use a CO_2 generator or tank to supplement if needed.

✓ **Pest and Disease Management:**

Implement integrated pest management (IPM) strategies to prevent and control pests and diseases.

Regularly inspect plants for signs of pests or diseases and take appropriate action promptly.

✓ **Security and Monitoring:**

Install security measures, such as locks, cameras, and alarms, to protect your grow space.

Use environmental monitors to track temperature, humidity, CO2 levels, and other crucial parameters.

✓ **Harvest and Processing Area:**

Allocate space for harvesting, drying, and curing your plants.

Ensure proper ventilation and humidity control in the processing area to maintain quality.

3. Lighting requirements for marijuana plants (LED, HPS, CMH)

✓ **LED Lights:**

Energy efficient: LED lights consume less energy compared to HPS and CMH lights, leading to lower electricity bills.

Spectrum control: LED lights can be tailored to provide specific light spectra suitable for different stages of plant growth, such as vegetative growth and flowering.

Heat management: LED lights produce less heat, reducing the need for additional cooling equipment in the grow room.

Long lifespan: LED lights have a longer lifespan compared to HPS and CMH lights, reducing the frequency of replacement.

✓ **HPS Lights:**

High light intensity: HPS lights produce high levels of light intensity, which is beneficial for flowering stages.

Cost-effective: HPS lights are relatively affordable compared to LED lights, making them a popular choice among growers.

Heat output: HPS lights generate a significant amount of heat, requiring adequate ventilation and cooling systems to maintain optimal temperatures in the grow room.

✓ **CMH Lights:**

Full spectrum: CMH lights provide a full spectrum of light that closely mimics natural sunlight, promoting healthy plant growth.

Efficiency: CMH lights are more efficient than HPS lights and produce less heat, making them a good choice for growers concerned about energy consumption and heat management.

Initial cost: CMH lights are generally more expensive than HPS lights, but their efficiency and spectrum quality can make them a worthwhile investment for some growers.

3. Ventilation and air circulation

Size and Type of Grow Space: Determine the size and layout of your grow room or tent to plan the ventilation system accordingly. Consider factors such as the number of plants, the type of cultivation method (e.g., hydroponic, soil), and the available space for equipment.

Air Exchange Rate: Calculate the required air exchange rate based on the size of your grow space. Aim for complete air exchange every 1 to 5 minutes, depending on factors like plant density, CO_2 supplementation, and temperature control needs.

Exhaust System: Install an exhaust system with a powerful fan to remove stale air, heat, and humidity from the grow space. Choose a fan size that can handle the volume of air in your grow room or tent.

Intake Air: Provide fresh intake air to replace the air being exhausted. Intake vents should be located near the bottom of the grow space to avoid recirculating warm, humid air from above.

Air Circulation Fans: Use oscillating fans inside the grow space to ensure even air distribution and to prevent stagnant air pockets. Position fans to create gentle airflow across the canopy without directly blowing on the plants.

Temperature and Humidity Control: Proper ventilation helps regulate temperature and humidity levels. Use inline fans with speed controllers or thermostats to adjust airflow based on environmental conditions.

CO_2 Enrichment: Consider CO_2 supplementation to enhance plant growth. Ensure that the ventilation system can distribute CO_2 evenly throughout the grow space.

Odor Control: Implement carbon filters in your exhaust system to eliminate odors. Replace filters regularly to maintain effectiveness.

Monitoring and Maintenance: Regularly monitor temperature, humidity, CO_2 levels, and airflow to ensure optimal conditions. Clean fans, filters, and ductwork periodically to prevent buildup of dust and contaminants.

4. Temperature and humidity control

✓ **Temperature:**

Ideal Range: The ideal temperature range for marijuana plants during the vegetative stage is 70-85°F (21-29°C) and during the flowering stage is 65-80°F (18-27°C).

Night Temperature Drop: A slight drop in temperature (about 10-15°F or 5-8°C) at night can mimic natural outdoor conditions and promote healthier growth.

Monitoring: Use a thermometer to monitor temperature levels consistently. Automated systems can help maintain precise control.

✓ **Humidity:**

Vegetative Stage: Aim for a humidity level of 40-70% during the vegetative stage to prevent issues like mold and mildew while promoting healthy growth.

Flowering Stage: Lower humidity to 40-50% during the flowering stage to reduce the risk of mold and encourage resin production.

Monitoring: Use a hygrometer to monitor humidity levels regularly. Dehumidifiers and humidifiers can help adjust humidity as needed.

✓ **Control Measures:**

Air Circulation: Good air circulation helps maintain uniform temperature and humidity levels throughout the grow space. Fans can be used for this purpose.

Ventilation: Proper ventilation helps remove excess heat and humidity. Consider exhaust fans and intake vents to regulate airflow.

Insulation: Insulate your grow room or tent to maintain stable temperatures and reduce energy costs.

Climate Controllers: Automated climate control systems can monitor and adjust temperature and humidity levels based on your pre-set parameters.

✓ **Avoiding Extremes:**

High Temperatures: High temperatures can lead to heat stress, reduced resin production, and increased risk of pests and diseases.

Low Humidity: Low humidity can cause plant stress, slow growth, and increase the risk of nutrient uptake issues.

Chapter 3

SOIL PREPARATION AND NUTRIENT MANAGEMENT

1.Selecting the right soil or growing medium (soil vs. hydroponics)Soil Cultivation

✓ **Soil Cultivation:**

Advantages:

Well-suited for beginners due to its forgiving nature and ease of use.

Provides a buffer for nutrient delivery, helping to maintain a stable pH level.

Organic soil can enhance the flavor and aroma of the final product.

Considerations:

Quality and composition of the soil are crucial. Look for well-draining, nutrient-rich soil with good aeration.

Regular soil amendments and fertilization may be needed to maintain nutrient levels.

Soil may harbor pests and diseases, requiring careful monitoring and management.

✓ **Hydroponic Cultivation:**

Advantages:

Allows for precise control over nutrient delivery, leading to potentially faster growth and higher yields.

Reduced risk of soil-borne pests and diseases.

Can be more water-efficient than soil cultivation.

Considerations:

Requires a good understanding of nutrient solutions and pH management.

Initial setup costs can be higher due to the need for hydroponic systems and equipment.

Requires regular monitoring and adjustments to nutrient levels and pH.

2. Soil testing for pH and nutrient levels

pH Testing: The pH level of your soil is a measure of its acidity or alkalinity. Marijuana plants thrive in slightly acidic soil with a pH range of 6.0 to 7.0. You can test the pH using a soil pH meter or a soil pH test kit. Follow the instructions provided with the meter or kit to collect soil samples from different areas of your growing area. Mix the samples thoroughly and test the pH according to the kit's instructions. Adjust the pH as needed by adding pH-adjusting products like lime to raise pH or sulfur to lower pH.

Nutrient Testing: Nutrient testing involves analyzing the levels of essential nutrients in your soil, such as nitrogen (N), phosphorus (P), potassium (K), calcium (Ca), magnesium (Mg), sulfur (S), iron (Fe), manganese (Mn), zinc (Zn), copper (Cu), boron (B), and molybdenum (Mo). You can conduct a basic nutrient test using a soil test kit or send your soil samples to a professional soil testing laboratory for a comprehensive analysis. The results will help you determine if your soil lacks any essential nutrients and guide you in applying fertilizers or amendments to correct deficiencies.

3. Organic vs. synthetic nutrients

✓ **Organic Nutrients:**

Pros:

Derived from natural sources like compost, fish emulsion, bone meal, and other organic materials.

Tend to be more sustainable and environmentally friendly.

Promote soil health and microbial activity, which can improve plant health in the long term.

Generally less likely to cause nutrient imbalances or salt buildup in the soil.

Cons:

Can be slower to release and may require microbial activity in the soil to break down and become available to plants.

Batch consistency can vary due to natural variability in organic materials.

May not provide as precise control over nutrient ratios compared to synthetic nutrients.

✓ **Synthetic Nutrients:**

Pros:

Precisely formulated to provide specific nutrient ratios, allowing for more precise control over plant nutrition.

Generally faster-acting, as the nutrients are readily available to plants.

Can be easier to use and require less monitoring compared to organic nutrients.

Cons:

Derived from chemical compounds, which can raise concerns about environmental impact and long-term soil health.

Overuse or improper application can lead to nutrient imbalances, salt buildup in the soil, and potential harm to beneficial soil microbes.

May not promote soil health and microbial activity as effectively as organic nutrients.

4. Nutrient deficiencies and how to address them

✓ **Nitrogen (N) Deficiency:**

Symptoms: Yellowing of lower leaves, starting from the tips and spreading inward, while new growth appears light green.

Solution: Apply a nitrogen-rich fertilizer to the soil or adjust your feeding schedule to provide more nitrogen.

✓ **Phosphorus (P) Deficiency:**

Symptoms: Dark green leaves with purple or red stems, slow growth, and older leaves may become dark green or purple and eventually die.

Solution: Use a phosphorus-rich fertilizer or bloom booster to increase phosphorus levels in the soil.

Potassium (K) Deficiency:

Symptoms: Yellowing or browning of leaf edges and tips, weak stems, and lower yields.

Solution: Use a potassium-rich fertilizer or supplement to correct the deficiency.

✓ **Calcium (Ca) Deficiency:**

Symptoms: New leaves may curl or twist, and older leaves may show yellow or brown spots that can progress to necrosis.

Solution: Add calcium supplements to the soil or use a foliar spray containing calcium.

✓ **Magnesium (Mg) Deficiency:**

Symptoms: Yellowing between leaf veins, which may progress to entire leaves turning yellow or red, while veins remain green.

Solution: Apply magnesium sulfate (Epsom salt) dissolved in water or use a magnesium-rich fertilizer.

✓ **Iron (Fe) Deficiency:**

Symptoms: Yellowing between leaf veins, while veins remain green (similar to magnesium deficiency, but veins are not affected).

Solution: Use an iron chelate supplement or foliar spray to increase iron levels.

✓ **Sulfur (S) Deficiency:**

Symptoms: Yellowing of new growth, starting from the tips and progressing inward, and leaves may become brittle.

Solution: Apply sulfur-containing fertilizers or supplements to correct the deficiency.

5. Watering techniques and irrigation systems

Hand Watering: This is the most basic method where you manually water the plants using a watering can, hose, or watering wand. It allows for precise control over the amount of water and can be suitable for smaller operations. However, it can be labor-intensive and time-consuming for larger setups.

Drip Irrigation: Drip systems deliver water directly to the base of each plant through a network of tubes and emitters. This method conserves water by minimizing evaporation and runoff and provides a consistent supply of water to the plants. It can be automated for ease of use and is suitable for both soil and hydroponic setups.

Flood and Drain (Ebb and Flow): This hydroponic technique involves flooding the growing area with nutrient solution and then draining it back into a reservoir. It provides a periodic watering cycle that mimics natural irrigation patterns and ensures thorough watering of the plants' root systems.

Sprinkler Irrigation: Sprinkler systems can be used for outdoor or greenhouse cultivation. They spray water over the plants in a uniform manner, covering a larger area. However, they can be less efficient than drip systems and may lead to water wastage through evaporation.

Aeroponics: In aeroponic systems, plants are grown in a mist or fog environment without the use of soil or a medium. Nutrient-rich water is misted directly onto the plant roots, providing high oxygen levels and efficient nutrient uptake. Aeroponics can be highly efficient but requires careful monitoring and maintenance.

Hydroponic Systems: Various hydroponic systems, such as nutrient film technique (NFT), deep water culture (DWC), and aeroponics, utilize water as the primary medium for delivering nutrients to the plants. These systems can be highly efficient and offer precise control over nutrient levels, pH, and water delivery.

Chapter 4

MARIJUANA PLANT CARE AND MAINTENANCE

1. Pruning and training techniques (topping, FIMing, LST)

Topping: Topping involves removing the top growth tip (the apical meristem) of the main stem, typically during the vegetative stage. This encourages the plant to grow multiple main colas instead of one, resulting in a bushier plant with more bud sites. To top a plant, use clean scissors or pruning shears to cut the stem just above a node where new branches will emerge.

FIMing (F*ck, I Missed): FIMing is a variation of topping that involves removing a portion of the apical meristem rather than the entire tip. This technique is less precise and can result in multiple shoots emerging from the cut site, leading to a bushier plant. To FIM a plant, pinch or cut off about

80% of the apical meristem, leaving some of it intact to stimulate lateral growth.

LST (Low Stress Training): LST involves gently bending and tying down branches to create a more even canopy and maximize light exposure to lower bud sites. This technique is usually performed during the vegetative stage when the plant is more flexible. By training the plant horizontally, you can promote more even growth and increase the number of bud sites. Use soft plant ties to avoid damaging the stems.

2. Pest and disease management

Integrated Pest Management (IPM): Implement an IPM approach that combines various strategies to manage pests and diseases effectively. This can include biological controls (e.g., beneficial insects), cultural practices (e.g., sanitation, crop rotation), mechanical controls (e.g., traps), and, if necessary, chemical controls (e.g., pesticides) as a last resort.

Regular Monitoring: Regularly inspect your plants for signs of pests and diseases. Early detection allows for prompt action, reducing the impact on your crop.

Quarantine: When introducing new plants or clones, quarantine them for a period to prevent the spread of pests and diseases to your entire crop.

Cleanliness: Maintain a clean growing environment by removing dead plant matter, fallen leaves, and debris. This reduces hiding places for pests and disease pathogens.

Air Circulation: Ensure good air circulation in your grow room or tent to discourage the development of mold and mildew, which thrive in stagnant conditions.

Temperature and Humidity Control: Monitor and control temperature and humidity levels to create an environment that is less favorable for pests and diseases. Most pests and pathogens have specific temperature and humidity ranges in which they thrive.

Natural Predators: Introduce beneficial insects like ladybugs, predatory mites, or nematodes to control pests biologically. These natural predators can help keep pest populations in check without the need for chemical interventions.

Resistant Varieties: Consider using cannabis strains that are naturally resistant to common pests and diseases prevalent in your region.

Organic Remedies: Utilize organic remedies such as neem oil, insecticidal soaps, and microbial sprays, which are effective against pests and diseases while minimizing environmental impact.

Record Keeping: Keep detailed records of pest and disease occurrences, treatments applied, and their effectiveness. This information can help you refine your pest and disease management strategies over time.

3. Monitoring plant health and growth

Visual Inspection: Regularly inspect your plants for signs of health issues such as yellowing leaves, wilting, discoloration, spots, pests, or unusual growth patterns. Look for signs of nutrient deficiencies or excesses.

pH and EC Monitoring: Measure the pH and electrical conductivity (EC) of your nutrient solution or soil regularly. Cannabis plants prefer a slightly acidic pH range of 5.5 to 6.5 for optimal nutrient uptake.

Nutrient Monitoring: Keep track of the nutrients you're feeding your plants and monitor for any signs of deficiencies or toxicities. Adjust nutrient levels based on plant growth stages and nutrient uptake patterns.

Watering and Irrigation: Monitor your watering schedule and ensure that plants are receiving adequate but not excessive water. Overwatering can lead to root rot, while underwatering can cause nutrient deficiencies and stunted growth.

Environmental Monitoring: Monitor environmental factors such as temperature, humidity, and CO_2 levels. Cannabis plants thrive in temperatures between 70-85°F (21-29°C) during the day and slightly cooler temperatures at night. Humidity levels should be kept between 40-60% during the vegetative stage and around 40-50% during the flowering stage.

Lighting: If you're using artificial lighting, monitor the intensity and distance of your lights from the plants. Adjust lighting schedules and heights based on the stage of growth to optimize photosynthesis and avoid light stress.

Growth Rate and Development: Keep track of the growth rate and development of your plants. Monitor how quickly they are growing, how well they are branching, and how many flowers they are producing. This can help you identify any issues early on and make necessary adjustments.

Recording and Documentation: Maintain a detailed record of your observations, including dates, plant health status, any treatments or adjustments made, and environmental conditions. This information can help you track trends over time and make informed decisions for future crops.

4. Environmental factors affecting plant growth (light, temperature, humidity)

Light: Light is one of the most critical factors for marijuana growth, as it drives photosynthesis, the process by which plants convert light energy into chemical energy (sugars) for growth. In indoor settings, artificial lighting is often used, with options like LED, HPS (High-Pressure Sodium), and CMH (Ceramic Metal Halide) lights. The intensity, duration, and spectrum of light influence plant growth and flowering. For vegetative growth, plants typically need 18-24 hours of light per day, while flowering plants may require a 12-hour light cycle to induce bud development.

Temperature: Temperature affects various aspects of plant growth, including metabolism, nutrient uptake, and flowering. Marijuana plants thrive in temperatures between 70-85°F (21-29°C) during the day and slightly cooler temperatures of about 60-70°F (15-21°C) at night. Extremes in temperature can stress plants, leading to stunted growth, reduced yields, and increased susceptibility to pests and diseases. Maintaining a stable temperature within the optimal range is crucial for healthy plant growth.

Humidity: Humidity levels impact transpiration (the process by which plants release water vapor through their leaves) and overall plant health. In the vegetative stage, marijuana plants prefer higher humidity levels (around 60-70%) to support vigorous growth. However, during the flowering stage, lower humidity levels (around 40-50%) are recommended to reduce the risk of mold and mildew, which can thrive in high humidity environments. Proper ventilation and humidity control systems, such as dehumidifiers and humidifiers, can help maintain optimal humidity levels throughout the growth cycle.

5. Harvesting timing and techniques

Timing: Harvesting timing varies depending on the strain and desired effects. Generally, you should harvest when the trichomes (small resin glands) on the buds change from clear to cloudy or amber. This indicates that the cannabinoids are at their peak potency. Use a magnifying tool to inspect the trichomes closely.

Appearance: Look for other signs of readiness, such as the color of the pistils (hairs on the buds). When most of the pistils have turned from white to a darker color (usually brown or red), it's a good indicator that the plant is ready for harvest.

Flush: Before harvest, it's advisable to flush the plants with pure water for about a week to remove any remaining nutrients from the soil or growing medium. This can improve the flavor and smoothness of the final product.

Cutting: Use sharp, clean scissors or pruning shears to cut the branches one at a time. Handle the buds carefully to avoid damaging the trichomes.

Trimming: After cutting, you'll need to trim the buds to remove excess leaves and stems. This can be done by hand or using trimming machines. The goal is to achieve a clean, manicured look.

Drying: Hang the trimmed buds upside down in a cool, dark, and well-ventilated area with moderate humidity (around 50-60%). This process can take 5-15 days, depending on the conditions and the size of the buds.

Curing: Once the buds are dry, they should be cured in glass jars for a few weeks to several months. This process helps to enhance the flavor, aroma, and smoothness of the buds by allowing them to slowly release moisture and develop their full potential.

Storage: Store the cured buds in airtight containers in a cool, dark place to preserve their quality. Avoid exposing them to light, heat, or moisture, as these can degrade the cannabinoids and terpenes.

Chapter 5

HARVESTING, DRYING, AND CURING MARIJUANA

1.Harvesting methods (whole plant vs. selective harvesting)

Whole Plant Harvesting: This method involves cutting down the entire plant at once, typically when it reaches the desired maturity level. The entire plant is then trimmed and processed for drying and curing. Whole plant harvesting is straightforward and efficient, especially for large-scale operations. It allows for a more uniform drying process since all parts of the plant are harvested together. However, it may not be suitable for strains with different maturity rates in different parts of the plant, as some parts might be overripe or underripe when harvested.

Selective Harvesting: In selective harvesting, only the mature buds or flowers are harvested while leaving the rest of the plant to continue growing. This method is more labor-intensive and time-consuming since it requires frequent inspections to identify and harvest ripe buds. Selective harvesting allows growers to harvest multiple times from the same plant, known as "phased harvesting," as the lower parts of the plant continue to develop new buds. It can result in higher overall yields and quality, as each bud is harvested at its peak ripeness. However, it requires more attention to detail and may not be as efficient for large-scale operations compared to whole plant harvesting.

2. Trimming and manicuring buds

Timing: Harvest your marijuana plants when the majority of the trichomes (the tiny resin glands on the buds) have turned milky white and some have started to turn amber. This is the peak time for cannabinoid and terpene production, which affects the potency and aroma of your buds.

Harvesting: Cut the branches with buds from the plant and remove any large fan leaves. Handle the buds gently to avoid damaging the trichomes.

Trimming: Use a pair of sharp, clean scissors or trimming shears to carefully trim away the sugar leaves (smaller leaves with trichomes) from the buds. The goal is to remove excess plant material while preserving the shape and structure of the buds. Some growers prefer a wet trim (trimming immediately after harvesting) while others prefer a dry trim (trimming after drying). Each method has its pros and cons, so choose what works best for your process and preferences.

Manicuring: After trimming, you can further manicure the buds by hand to remove any remaining small leaves or stems. This step helps improve the appearance and overall quality of the buds. Take care not to handle the buds too much, as excessive touching can transfer oils from your hands and affect the flavor and aroma.

Drying and Curing: Once trimmed and manicured, hang the buds in a cool, dark, and well-ventilated space to dry. After drying, you can further enhance the flavor, aroma, and smoothness of your buds through a process called curing. Place the dried buds in airtight containers (like glass jars) and store them in a cool, dark place with controlled humidity levels for several weeks to allow the flavors and aromas to develop.

Quality Control: Throughout the trimming and manicuring process, it's important to inspect the buds for any signs of mold, mildew, or pests. Proper hygiene and cleanliness are essential to maintain the quality and purity of your final product.

3. Drying marijuana buds (drying racks, humidity levels)

Drying Racks: Use drying racks or mesh screens to hang the buds. Make sure the racks are in a well-ventilated, dark, and dry room. Avoid overcrowding the racks to allow air circulation around the buds.

Humidity Levels: Maintain a humidity level of around 45-55% during the drying process. High humidity can lead to mold growth, while low humidity can cause the buds to dry too quickly, affecting their quality.

Monitoring Humidity: Use a hygrometer to monitor the humidity levels in the drying room. Adjust the humidity by increasing or decreasing ventilation or using dehumidifiers if needed.

Drying Time: The drying process typically takes 7-14 days, depending on factors like humidity, temperature, and bud size. Buds are ready when the stems snap easily but still have some moisture inside.

Temperature: Maintain a temperature of around 60-70°F (15-21°C) for optimal drying. Avoid high temperatures, as they can cause the buds to dry too quickly and lose potency.

Darkness: Keep the drying room dark to protect the buds from light, which can degrade cannabinoids and terpenes.

Checking Buds: Regularly check the buds for signs of mold, mildew, or over-drying. Remove any damaged or moldy buds immediately to prevent further contamination.

4. Curing marijuana buds (jar curing, burping)

Drying the Buds: After harvesting, dry your buds in a dark, well-ventilated area with a temperature of around 60-70°F (15-21°C) and a humidity level of 45-55%. This process can take 5-15 days depending on the size and density of your buds.

Jar Curing: Once the buds are dry but still slightly moist on the inside (usually when the stems snap rather than bend), transfer them to clean, airtight glass jars. Fill the jars about 3/4 full to leave some air space.

Burping: During the first week of jar curing, you'll need to "burp" the jars daily to release any excess moisture and prevent mold growth. Open the jars for a few minutes each day to allow fresh air to circulate.

Monitoring: After the first week, you can reduce the frequency of burping to once every few days.

Monitor the buds for signs of mold or excessive moisture. If you notice any, remove the affected buds immediately.

Duration: Continue the jar curing process for at least 2-4 weeks, or even longer for optimal results. The longer you cure, the smoother and more flavorful your buds will become.

Storage: Once the curing process is complete, you can store your cured buds in a cool, dark place in airtight containers to preserve their quality.

5. Testing for potency and quality control

Potency Testing: This involves measuring the concentration of cannabinoids, such as THC (tetrahydrocannabinol) and CBD (cannabidiol), in the harvested buds. High-performance liquid chromatography (HPLC) or gas chromatography (GC) are commonly used methods to analyze cannabinoid levels. Testing can also include other cannabinoids and terpenes, which contribute to the overall effect and aroma of the cannabis.

Quality Control: This encompasses various tests and checks to ensure the overall quality of the product. This can include:

Microbial Testing: To detect the presence of harmful bacteria, molds, yeast, or other microorganisms that could affect the safety and shelf life of the product.

Pesticide Residue Testing: To ensure that the cannabis is free from harmful pesticide residues, which can be hazardous to consumers.

Heavy Metal Testing: To check for the presence of heavy metals like lead, mercury, cadmium, and arsenic, which can be absorbed by the plant from the soil and pose health risks if present in high concentrations.

Moisture Content Testing: To determine the moisture level in the buds, which is important for proper curing and storage to prevent mold growth.

Foreign Matter Inspection: Visual inspection or sieving to ensure that the product is free from contaminants such as dirt, insects, or other foreign materials.

Potency and Quality Control Labs: Many jurisdictions require cannabis products to undergo testing at accredited laboratories before they can be sold. These labs use standardized methods and equipment to ensure accurate and reliable results.

Compliance: It's essential to ensure that your marijuana business complies with local regulations regarding testing requirements. This includes adhering to testing frequencies, methods, and reporting standards mandated by the regulatory authorities.

Record Keeping: Keeping detailed records of all testing results is crucial for quality control and compliance purposes. This documentation helps track the potency and quality of your products over time and provides transparency to regulators and consumers.

Chapter 6

MARKETING AND SELLING YOUR MARIJUANA

1. Understanding the legal and regulatory requirements for selling marijuana

Licensing and Permits: Most jurisdictions require businesses involved in the cultivation, processing, distribution, or sale of marijuana to obtain licenses or permits. These licenses often have specific requirements and application processes, including background checks and compliance with security measures.

Legalization Status: Check the legal status of marijuana in your area. Some places have fully legalized marijuana for both medical and recreational use, while others may only allow medical use or have stricter regulations.

Age Restrictions: In areas where marijuana is legal, there are typically age restrictions for purchasing and using it. Make sure you understand the minimum age requirements and comply with them.

Product Testing and Labeling: Many jurisdictions require marijuana products to undergo testing for potency, purity, and contaminants. Proper labeling with accurate information about the product's contents and potency is also usually mandatory.

Taxes and Fees: Be aware of the taxes and fees associated with selling marijuana. These can include excise taxes, sales taxes, and licensing fees, which can vary depending on the type of marijuana business and your location.

Security and Record-Keeping: Security requirements, such as surveillance systems and secure storage, are often mandated to prevent theft and diversion. Additionally, maintaining detailed records of your business operations and transactions is usually required for regulatory compliance.

Advertising and Marketing Restrictions: Many jurisdictions have strict rules regarding the advertising and marketing of marijuana products. This can include limitations on where and how you can advertise, as well as restrictions on the content of your marketing materials.

Compliance with Local Zoning Laws: Ensure that your business location complies with local zoning laws and regulations related to marijuana businesses. There may be specific zoning requirements or restrictions on where you can operate.

Transportation and Distribution: If you are involved in the distribution or transportation of marijuana products, there may be additional regulations regarding how products are transported, stored, and delivered.

Employee Training and Compliance: Training employees on compliance with relevant laws and regulations is essential. They should be knowledgeable about age restrictions, product information, and proper handling of marijuana products.

2. Developing a branding strategy

Define Your Brand Identity: Start by defining your brand's unique identity, including your mission, values, and what sets you apart from competitors. Consider the image you want to portray and the emotions you want to evoke in your customers.

Target Audience: Identify your target audience and understand their needs, preferences, and lifestyle. Tailor your brand messaging and visuals to appeal to this specific demographic.

Brand Name and Logo: Choose a memorable and distinctive brand name that reflects your values and resonates with your target audience. Design a logo that visually represents your brand and is easily recognizable.

Brand Story: Develop a compelling brand story that communicates your journey, values, and commitment to quality. This can help build a connection with your customers and differentiate your brand in the market.

Brand Voice and Messaging: Define your brand voice, including the tone and language you use in your communications. Ensure consistency across all touchpoints, from marketing materials to customer interactions.

Visual Identity: Create a cohesive visual identity that includes colors, fonts, and imagery that align with your brand's personality and appeal to your target audience.

Packaging and Labeling: Design packaging and labels that not only comply with legal requirements but also reflect your brand's identity and values. Consider sustainability and eco-friendly options if they align with your brand image.

Marketing and Communication Channels: Identify the most effective marketing channels to reach your target audience, such as social media, influencer marketing, and industry events. Develop a content strategy that showcases your brand's expertise and engages your audience.

Customer Experience: Focus on delivering a consistent and exceptional customer experience that reinforces your brand values. This includes everything from product quality to customer service interactions.

Feedback and Adaptation: Continuously gather feedback from customers and monitor market trends to adapt your branding strategy as needed. Stay flexible and open to evolving your brand to meet changing consumer preferences.

3. Packaging and labeling requirements

Child-Resistant Packaging: Cannabis products are often required to be packaged in child-resistant containers to prevent accidental ingestion by children. These containers should meet specific standards set by regulatory authorities.

Product Information: Labels must include essential product information such as the product name, THC/CBD content, net weight, serving size, and total servings. Some jurisdictions may also require the inclusion of other cannabinoids, terpenes, and their respective percentages.

Warnings and Statements: Mandatory warnings and statements, such as "Keep out of reach of children," "For use only by adults 21 and older," and "Cannabis may impair your ability to drive and operate machinery. Use with caution," are often required.

Ingredients List: A list of ingredients used in the product, including any allergens or other substances of concern, should be provided.

Batch Number and Expiry Date: Each product should have a batch number and expiry date to track its production and ensure consumer safety.

Testing Information: Some jurisdictions require cannabis products to undergo testing for potency, pesticides, heavy metals, and microbial contaminants. The label may need to include information about the testing laboratory and results.

Dosage and Usage Instructions: If applicable, the label should include dosage instructions and recommended use.

Manufacturer Information: The label should include the name and contact information of the manufacturer or distributor.

QR Code or Barcode: Some jurisdictions require products to have a QR code or barcode for tracking and verification purposes.

4. Distribution channels (dispensaries, online sales)

Dispensaries: These are physical retail stores where customers can purchase marijuana products. Dispensaries can be standalone stores or part of larger cannabis retail chains. They often offer a variety of products, including flower, edibles, concentrates, and more.

Online Sales: Selling marijuana products online can be a convenient way to reach customers who prefer to shop from home. This can be done through your own e-commerce website or through online marketplaces that specialize in cannabis products. Keep in mind that online sales may be subject to additional regulations and restrictions, depending on your location.

Wholesale: Selling your products to other businesses, such as dispensaries or processors, on a wholesale basis can be a significant part of your distribution strategy. This allows you to reach a broader market without directly dealing with retail sales.

Delivery Services: Some regions allow for the delivery of cannabis products directly to customers' homes. This can be a convenient option for customers who may not have easy access to a physical dispensary.

Collaborations and Partnerships: Partnering with other businesses in the cannabis industry, such as brands that offer complementary products or services, can help expand your reach and attract new customers.

5. Customer education and support

Product Knowledge: Provide detailed information about your marijuana products, including strain types, cannabinoid profiles (e.g., THC, CBD), terpene profiles, and potential effects. Educate customers on how to select products based on their preferences and needs.

Dosage and Consumption Methods: Educate customers on proper dosage guidelines and various consumption methods (e.g., smoking, vaping, edibles, topicals). Highlight the importance of starting with low doses and gradually increasing to avoid overconsumption.

Health and Safety: Emphasize the importance of responsible consumption and the potential risks associated with marijuana use, especially for certain populations (e.g., pregnant women, individuals with certain medical conditions). Provide guidance on storing marijuana products safely away from children and pets.

Legal and Regulatory Compliance: Ensure that customers are aware of the legal and regulatory requirements related to marijuana consumption, including age restrictions, possession limits, and where it is legal to consume.

Customer Support: Offer reliable customer support channels (e.g., helpline, email, chat) for addressing customer inquiries, concerns, and feedback. Provide prompt and accurate responses to build trust and loyalty.

Educational Resources: Develop educational materials such as pamphlets, videos, or online guides that cover topics like cultivation methods, strain selection, and product quality. Host workshops or webinars to engage customers and provide in-depth knowledge.

Community Engagement: Create a community around your brand where customers can share their experiences, tips, and knowledge about marijuana cultivation and consumption. Encourage discussions and peer-to-peer support.

Continuous Learning: Stay updated with the latest research, trends, and regulations in the marijuana industry to provide accurate and relevant information to your customers.